LOVE SOULFUL BITES

UDAIGIRI AMARAVATHI

FanatiXx Publication
https://fanatixxpublication.com

FanatiXx Publication
AM/56, Basanti Colony, Rourkela 769012, Odisha
ISO 9001:2015 Certified

© Copyright, 2023

All rights reserved. No part of this book may be reproduced, stored in a retrieval system, or transmitted, in any form by any means, electronic, mechanical, magnetic, optical, chemical, manual, photocopying, recording, or otherwise, without the prior written consent of the author.

By: Udaigiri Amaravathi
ISBN: 978-93-5605-153-9
Cover Design: Sagar Chand Samal
Price: INR 149/-
Print and typeset by: BooksClub.in

The opinions/ contents expressed in this book are the sole of the author and do not represent the opinions/ stands/ thoughts of FanatiXx® or any of its associates and affiliations.

Disclaimer

All rights reserved. This book may not be reproduced in whole or in part, or transmitted in any form, without written permission from the publisher, nor may any part of this book be reproduced, stored in a retrieval system, or transmitted in any form or by any means electronic, mechanical, photocopying, microfilming, and recording without written permission from the publisher.

Author assures that all content is original and he/she has full rights to publish and distribute the same. In any case of plagiarism, the publisher is not liable.

Acknowledgement

To all the individuals I have had the opportunity to lead, be led by, or watch their work of excellence from afar, I want to say thank you for being the inspiration and foundation for this piece of art that you surely have to imbibe and imprint in your hearts and souls with love and cherish it presenting it to your loved ones.

This pleasing, painful and also pleasurable literary outcome wasn't possible without the experiences and support from my peers and team of FanatiXx Publications. Special thanks to the greatest of great poets i.e Jonne Donne for giving all the love through his poems from whom I needed inspiration to write this Literary compilation of poems and also to "you know who" & my family for bearing me through the whole process.

Udaigiri Amaravathi is an enthusiastic writer, a post graduate in English Literature and a resident of Land of Nizam's - the Hyderabad City, who started off her writing journey with one of the most beautiful Erotic poetic work in Fantasy fiction & Romance genre called "Unquenchable desires" in her early 20's which was published in March, 2020.

Her first book received literary accolades from the readers that paved her a new path which made to explore herself in writing a Soulful short story named "Barren Land of Love" which is a part of an Anthology book of Short story compilations called "Strength from Darkness". Her works fetched her Best Budding Author's award from FanatiXx Spectrum Awards in 2021 and 21st Century Emily

Dickinson's award in early 2022. She is greatly inspired by metaphysical poetic collections of the greatest English poets John Donne & is currently aspiring to add a tinge of his flavors constructively in her poems.

Instagram Handle : Udaigiri.echoes
Mail Id : learnwithmammu@gmail.com

Contents:

Disclaimer... iii
Acknowledgement iv
About v
1. Smiling Scars... 2
2. Drowning Identity....................................... 4
3. Rhythm of Hearts.. 6
4. Chores of Sorrow Heart 8
5. Dimensions of madness 10
6. Courage to confess...................................... 12
7. Rooting in trials 14
8. The raining darkness................................... 16
9. Addictive Delight. 18
10. Endless crime.. 20
11. Love Consequence.................................... 22
12. Elixir of you.. 24
13. Heaven of Care 26
14. Ship Unsinkable.. 28
15. Heart Lanes... 30
16. His mere sight... 32
17. No longer put to lie 34
18. Paradise of trust 36
19. Decision so fair... 38
20. Union of lips 40
21. Monsoon Ages.. 42

22. Heartfelt gain 44
23. Dart of Sight 46
24. Epoch of love 48
25. Love Duet 50
26. Togetherness and Trust 52
27. Alluring Soul 54
28. Aisle of heart 56
29. Mystic Dawn 58
30. Oasis of Serenity 60

~~Love~~ Soulful Bites

"When I am in search of long-lost happiness under the shadows of tears, that is refusing to reflect my agony."

1. Smiling Scars

The bitterness of fury might never seem to settle its wrath,
My inevitable trail to halt this dreadful collapse loses its path,
Those bleeding old music & smiling scars plant me somewhere,
This whirlpool of silly plays seems hard to bear.

I question myself, "How do I pull over this survival game & thrive?"
Stabbed & broken dozens of times but still, this heart is alive.
Couldn't I be spared to unbarred & forgo the regret?
Every day turns null & void with such disgust on my calendar.

I doubted my existence like the seasons of autumn leaf shed,
The hopes & faith in life spilled over like slaughtered blood,
Let the joy of laughter betray my wrath of sorrows,
I wish to owe the beauty to beset in me every today and tomorrow.

~~Love~~ Soulful Bites

"The flesh I live in is beyond the vicinity of blame. Unknown how to play this winner's game."

2. Drowning Identity

The reflection of pain hasn't been addressed,
Fleeting like a shadow, the past often commences,
The battlefield of innocence never seems to be gone,
Not allowing the wrath to be forgotten and reckoned.

These shackles of nightmares stumbled in the dark,
Drowning my identity into uneven and void thoughts.
Have I got these gorgeous scars upon my insist?
Why that is a human life cannot forgo and resist?

A page of chapter equipped with the heart of warriors,
Without any glance of intimation and broken barriers,
Those fragments of forgotten images roll over in my brain,
Never let me pass through the happiness lane.

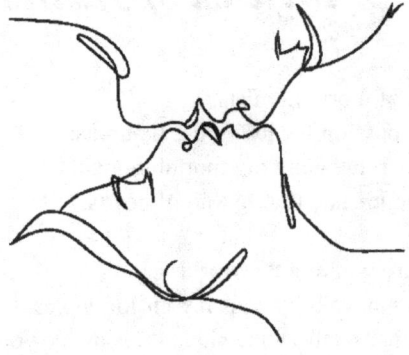

"Yet again we skipped, but I shall hold you tight to create an abode of love and light."

3. Rhythm of Hearts

In the mellows of morning mists,
There's a clear passion for living life that exists,
Forfeiting the darkness and my mortal thoughts,
I enjoy this solitude and the rhythm of hearts.

It doesn't require winning the world,
It just is you that have to vanquish your loopholes,
Perhaps, you must swallow the silent cries inside you!
Because you are the precious one God made out of very few.

Severe those pestering ties and set yourself free,
Let your spirits fly, glide and float like a sea...
The momentum of strength and emotions is all that you need,
Life begs you only a little for an exceptional lead.

~~Love~~ Soulful Bites

"No feeling is forever. But, a culprit of our own torments."

4. Chores of Sorrow Heart

That lingering form I can't touch is filled with my essence,
It seems like a shadow of a non-existing presence,
Why do I fall every time and wonder?
I was once yours and some part of me still remains under!

Learned from the waves of unspeakable agony and beautiful struggles,
Want to make trials to stand in their own thoughts and fight obstacles,
Weeping and sobbing for all the odds drilled in memories crust,
I feel like pausing the time and stealing you from the past.

I will make sure to watch over the premises of my heart again,
And swear to never drive into the negativity of life and drain,
Emotions got hijacked and nerves started playing their part,
Finally God, I have learned to deal with chores of sorrow heart.

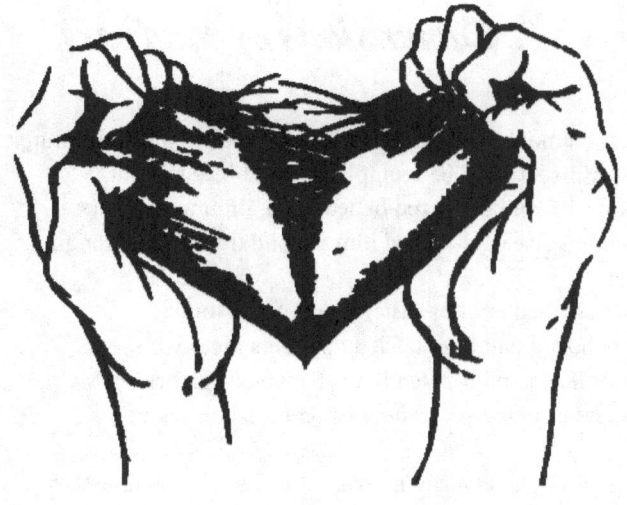

"How could I escape this passion plight because he seized my heart with his mere sight."

5. Dimensions of madness

Shot upon me those feeble practices to do the embrace killing,
I saw his beautiful face crumple in cold blue starlight,
His track of walks faltered beneath the glimmering stars,
Something else crystallized him beyond the tethered longing.

Words escaped my lips faster than I could think,
Voice choked and throat dried up on his mere wink,
Eyes widened and blinked to exchange our glances of sight,
Whispers of new love trailed off on that dark night.

Spirits slowly fade away in every dimension of madness,
Unraveling thoughts of love began to vent and confess,
Embracing his undaunted look, my feet started slipping,
Those worldly distances between us were set to condense…

~~Love~~ Soulful Bites

"To unfold those crumpled pages of the past, he entered my life to add new chapters of love."

6. Courage to confess

Underneath those flairs of crimson red sunset of the moon,
I have noticed a man in the evenings of bustling monsoon.
I realized I have been in a long hibernation sleep,
In front of me was a dream farm harvest so reap.

The moment got seized in sight of each other's vows,
Thoughts dared to venture into the dream of clouds.
I solemnly got embarked into the world of bonding currents,
But never I regretted losing myself in the illusion fronts.

The winds have begun to lull around my ears,
Suggesting my soul not to have any more fears,
Trying to understand the scrambled ideas of mess,
I made up my mind and heart to gain the courage to confess.

~~Love~~ Soulful Bites

"Handling the chaos all alone. Don't you draw your conclusions on your own."

Udaigiri Amaravathi

7. Rooting in trials

Standing and aiming his arrows at his foe,
Distorted emotions and agony of pain grow,
The world made him suffer pangs of anxiety,
He couldn't understand the inebriated society.

He was devoid of love and is rendered barren,
He needed a shoulder to amend his sorrow & let the tears drain,
The protest with its chaos seems to never end,
Between these rivals, the hope of my love ascends.

His resonant voice kept me engaged,
Absorbed in mind, his thoughts got caged,
I disturbed his prayers and added a new one,
witnessed him rooting in trials until it was done.

~~Love~~ Soulful Bites

"His silence sounded louder than the hustle of crowds. His tears stroke his cheeks like rumbling thunders."

8. The raining darkness

With the raining darkness from the heavens, there seems no god to rise before this prison,
But don't you judge so early, there is always beauty to listen.
He wants to vent out those dark secrets hidden underneath him,
Those kisses of thankfulness were adored on his chin.

Tell me something, "What takes it to put you down and frown?"
Every arm needs a caring man and a woman of a crown.
Subtle selfishness seems to be hidden under his every pain,
He needs comfort and a soothing head to explain.

The laughing devils are trying to shovel his self-confidence,
The pages of rage are blank but yet to be filled with self-defense.
A man's masculinity isn't measured by multiple mating partners,
His real self comes out from his character apparatus.

~~Love~~ Soulful Bites

"Let me lay on your chest every night where all the dancing angels and grinning demons try to separate our hug so tight."

9. Addictive Delight.

Skies and oceans giggle watching his laughs and smiles,
Even stars drizzle and the shower glitters at his gaze from million miles.
"What is he made of?" I wonder and fascinate,
He is one such thought that I love to procrastinate.

Bonding with him is my soul's representation and royal,
Thumping my every organ and every cell to accomplish the ideal.
His cold sight can keep me warm throughout the night,
and his affable arms could stand as an addictive delight.

Gosh! I feel like the heavens are blessing me more these days,
He shall be gifted with all the love of this world and caress,
How can I get a man of enchanting beauty with such delay?
A crownless prince with a lovely soul is all I witnessed.

~~Love~~ Soulful Bites

"When I had more to confide in, he shared my loneliness."

10. Endless crime

I remember all those sights,
When the sun blew out of his smile…
I owe to implement an endless crime,
watching him out in my dreams every time.

Feeling sprung to emotional bonds,
As if he pulled the new rhythm of cords.
I heard those echoes thumping in my valves,
Pupils dilate on his wondrous fair palps.

As he moved through those undulating grass fields,
impulses aroused slowly into the lights of things…
Cast around breaking away every bar,
Left imprinting away those reasonless scars.

~~Love~~ Soulful Bites

"Yes, I have witnessed a man; the real one indeed. He is the man of my life."

11. Love Consequence

In the pursuit of knowing unhidden truth,
Rugged inside the naked primal youth.
Between the groping hearts and wailing winds,
He owes to give me every possible hint.

Looking deep into his peering eyes,
He seemed undaunted & more of a man.
Wrapped up my mind in his jazzy madness,
In a situation stuck with no escape entrance.

Beyond the crest of the world, I searched for wild bliss,
Streamed through my concerns, my soul out-poured for his excitable kiss.
Overflowed with passionate grand gestures of lengths,
love pavements arouse leading to a new consequence.

"I can't help but ignite my senses with hope. A rotten hope that he might turn to me."

12. Elixir of you

You pit wits against me and make me vulnerable,
I examine myself, why am I turning so unpredictable?
Diseased by various doubts and contagious thoughts,
I call upon to gods, between those drowning hearts.

The desire is so bleak and lame that's failing to heal,
Pierced are my heart walls shot by the angels.
Damn! I often dare to swim in the pool of revival,
The longing love awaits to turn into your victim of oblivion.

Unblessed, am I? If I don't frail in the love of mirth and sin,
What will be the use of this wicked win?
Death shall kiss me through....
If I am not gifted with the elixir of you.

~~Love~~ Soulful Bites

"Waiting for the oceans of sorrow to fade. My broken heart now seems to heal with a bunch of band-aids."

13. Heaven of Care

The stumbling walks of mine are now retrieving their balances,
The memories of despair are slowly escaping my senses,
You draped my crazy world of wild fantasies to perfectly align,
And fetched enough courage to fight all odds and made me feel fine.

You are that sweet stench of venom, I am ready to get doped,
Because you run all my worldly illusions turn into new hope,
I started slipping into the dark naps of twirling twilights,
beheld by you in your arms so warm and tight.

You came like a blazing sun into my midnight skies,
turned into a star of strength before my weakened breath dies,
Now, I endeavor every minute to breathe to make my life fair,
Also, my soul drowning to die in your heaven of care....

~~Love~~ Soulful Bites

"For once, let me free from all problems, for once let me flee in your heavenly arms."

14. Ship Unsinkable

Enclose me tight in those pretty eyes,
Quench my thirst in your arms so nice,
You run wild in my little mind,
The reason for this admiration is because you are my kind.

My thoughts walk an extra mile with affection that springs forth,
Busily looking for you to merge me in soulful warmth,
My inner peace seems to be intruded with your love again and again,
The dark ambiance of night skies drove me into the eternal zen.

Sticking to your thoughts is beyond my levels of saturation,
Oh, Lord! Save me from this crazy killing mesmerization,
Lost my conscience to that crush unimaginable,
Propelling my love waves in a ship unsinkable.

~~Love~~ Soulful Bites

"My love transited from flawed to flawless. Drove over my thoughts like dancing dew droplets."

15. Heart Lanes

They say love is so uncertain and messy pool of trap nets,
But I feel they didn't cherish for sure the essence of true love yet,
Don't you please try to acquire love as your goal and share?
It's all about, how you shower your compassion and care.

I don't trust and believe in the theory of the next lives,
All I have got to do is to die in your arms and stay alive,
Let my soul dwell within you without hinting at my absence,
We shall experience the paradise of love and its pleasance.

If I burn into ashes, don't collect my remains,
But, instead, live and travel all through my heart lanes,
Don't sob and never let your emotions shake,
I shall come into your dreams to make your smiles awake.

"He shines upon my face, making my days turn so bright."

16. His mere sight

The sun must have borrowed all his shine,
Letting all the glories and chandeliers decline,
The moon must have shaken to death,
Watching your smiles and laughter beneath.

Shadows hideaway, as if they lost their life now,
Thunders rumble in jealous of his charm that flows,
Stars drew their brightening lights to surrender before him,
On his one mere sight, my whole world turns so dim.

Even the nightingales couldn't catch his gleeful tunes,
For his heart which waited for me in midnight monsoons,
God must be proud of making such flawless hearts,
His every move is enough to hit many hearts like darts.

~~Love~~ Soulful Bites

"He kissed me with his prayers and embraced me with his honesty."

17. No longer put to lie

He stole the moons glow in between those emerging dark,
Letting my soul inherit the stirring flow of emotions,
Those strands of waving hair and twisted muscles,
Tell me there is more to explore in the man you love.

His blissful arms leaned towards me to caress and love, giving all the warmth,
Our souls are free from the ache of freedom and
our eyes are no longer put to lie,
What life is it? If every moment is not destined to die for him.

The hair on his heart is calling my fingers to twirl over,
Those lustrous lips are waiting to bite my neck so tender,
Those shallow rivers and foggy nights are not endless & left unknown,
where we don't have to fight to put on fake smile and frown.

~~Love~~ Soulful Bites

"Let me stain your shirt with my tears of cry. Let me stain your lips with my bites of joy."

18. Paradise of trust

What brings you to the border of my domain,
We drenched and danced in the enchanting rain,
Love is an unpredictable journey they say,
This paradise of our trust may never fail I pray.

Break the rules and pinch off my sorrow,
Let me wake up in your arms every now and tomorrow,
I shall promise to grieve your every pain,
And will rejoice in the memories of our beautiful remains.

Try not to break my heart, Oh! my dear lovely love,
I want us to be apart from all these pathos above,
I shall promise to bestow the best of my true self,
Till you crave for every bit of my presence engulf.

~~Love~~ Soulful Bites

"Words would make no sense to me when I can hear the lingering beats of his heart."

19. Decision so fair

The wind carried all the silence of his gaze,
The sky opened its door to the heavenly rains,
He tilted his neck to gasp his warm breaths,
When his ears heard the faint whisper.

Caressed over the strands of my hair,
Realizing that I made a decision fair,
He cradled my soul and put my heart to sleep,
His emotions and love for which I am falling deep.

I felt like we are no less than warriors,
Deceiving ourselves and conquering all the world,
We would love, apologize and live again in acquaintance,
Together this bond shines until its existence.

~~Love~~ Soulful Bites

"The air between us was gasping to escape and the kiss of our love made all the gods communicate."

20. Union of lips

How can I miss remembering,
That three-hour-long kiss locked in my mind and my calendar,
Keeping all the hesitation and insecurity at bay,
Love and hormonal reactions paved their way.

We still were unaware whether we closed the door,
He pushed me against the wall to relish me more,
Union of lips was the only goal to reach and important,
I lost my appetite and my existence at that very moment.

Loop of different worlds revolved through my head,
Craving to taste the soul of love and honor on the bed,
Be it the last day of the year or the beginning of the new year,
My lips kept smiling realizing it every night Oh! My dear.

"Like a rainbow after the rain, he doped my heart with joy from every soulful pain."

21. Monsoon Ages

In the mellow of monsoon ages,
There's a quench of thirst to reduce all our space,
We will drench in the rains all over,
Water will drip from all your curls to your shoulders.

To taste every wriggling droplet on your curves,
My tongue will twirl to quiver all your nerves.
The sun shall hide to save us from solitude,
And the clouds will bound up to cover our bodies nude.

I will need many lives to venture into your beautiful body,
And hide you from every evil eye don't you worry,
You made my heavens fall apart with your ace,
Every bit of myself un left leaving no trace.

~~Love~~ Soulful Bites

"His love covered everything and erased my tears; turned my barren land into a garden of flowers."

22. Heartfelt gain

Those black clouds covered us underneath,
Cuddling us under monsoon-rich sheath,
Those peacock yells and twitter chirps,
Those soulful hugs and kisses slurp.

I was in the arms of nature's soul,
Rugged under the care of his love control,
Emissions of the sun missed its fury,
I stole the shine of the humble moon story.

Speaking to the serenity of cloudy night,
I kissed him deep and held him tight,
The dizziness of booze drove me insane,
Cheers and kudos to myself for this heartfelt gain.

~~Love~~ Soulful Bites

"Hug me tight, until I begin to smell like you."

23. Dart of Sight

Swept off my soul those unheard tunes,
Witnessed when I your ineffable demilune form,
The pendant on your chest is hidden beneath the crests,
Thriving for the want of your enduring lusts.

Suspended pearls are your sweat adorn,
Fill up my heart with the thirst unknown,
You must be the outcome of the yearn I impugn,
Dwelled in the love of creator in maple shed June.

Wanting to taste the nectar till the new moon,
Hit to the chores your dart of sight like a harpoon,
I will relish your every edge without any hustle,
Until I persuade your fondant figure with ease and supple.

~~Love~~ Soulful Bites

"I sailed through the drift of his dreams. Let me be the sailor of his ship."

24. Epoch of love

Scraping for warmth I met this boy,
To express my sorrows and my joy,
With lips so close to mutate distance and deliver,
I found a shoulder to lean on and whisper.

His quiet words lurk around my head,
I rewind his episodes of talks before going to bed,
To listen to his stories and spill my feelings,
Illuminates my every night and leaves me dreaming.

The places we have been and things we believe in,
The sky will witness how bounded we both are and loving,
The boredom of thoughts and emotions elapsed,
Wounds of past affinity now seem to be lost.

~~Love~~ Soulful Bites

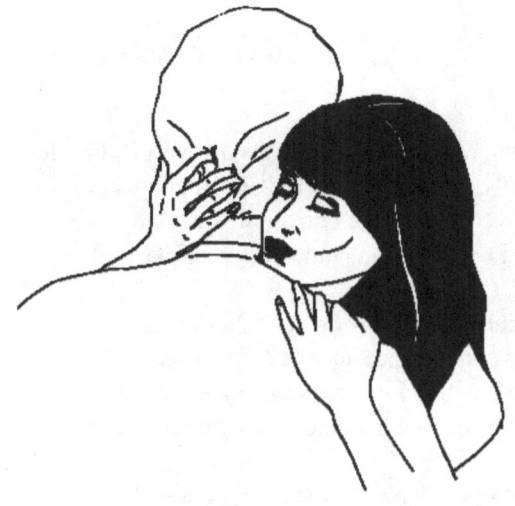

"The symphony among us can make me sing the songs of love till death."

25. Love Duet

History shall remind us someday as the world's best lovers,
The butterfly seems indebted to your laughing colors,
And the firefly must have borrowed your flawless grace,
There must be none who could take your place.

I saw the sun shining low on your cheeks,
Not to let your elegance and charm decrease,
Maybe the moon too started frowning at your light,
It must be aware that it's below your stardom tonight.

Our union was conspired by this whole world,
Even gods and goddesses were invited and told,
To come across this enchanting beauty of love duet,
And to sing the songs of love we would never forget.

~~Love~~ Soulful Bites

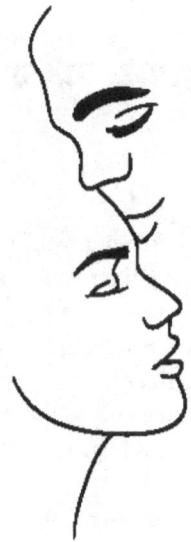

"Fragmented souls are now joining their ends, till all the love is consumed and passion deepens."

Udaigiri Amaravathi

26. Togetherness and Trust

Drag me to your side,
Love me like it's your right.
Barge into my heart & pierce it down,
My spirits & my soul that I'll let you own.

Let me fly in your arms like a feather of delight,
Kiss me slow & hug me tight.
Flourish through every inch and cell of me,
You don't have to wait until I agree.

We will dine until your lips are on mine,
I wish to praise your curves in my every poetry line.
Let's not leave even a fragment and trace of us,
Dwelling deep into the charms of togetherness & trust.

~~Love~~ Soulful Bites

"The mirages of happiness are no more an illusion. I've achieved you when mortality was the only solution."

27. Alluring Soul

When the whole world is wrapped under the hustle of city lights,
My soul is seemed by your lovely sight,
In the lap of nature so calm and pretty,
Away from the people and the noises of the city.

My wounds were lighter and so did my heart,
Dwelling under the shadow of your love art,
Stay with me dear all day long,
Arresting your alluring soul in me that's where I belong.

Hug me and tell me that you love me too,
Affirm me with your kisses that you'll cherish me through,
your entry into my life has made some sense to my existence,
years have brought me back to your passionate elegance.

~~Love~~ Soulful Bites

"Sparkling eyes and a fear that dies. Look above. A whole new chapter of life, but the same old love ignites."

28. Aisle of heart

Tell me your pathos; I can hear you cry,
Narrate me things that are biting your soul and restricting you to fly,
Let me kiss you and caress you forever my dear,
You can pour out your tears into my river.

Let the waves of your rage & agony be merged into my shores,
Do discover my love waiting for your walk into the aisle of my heart doors,
Wars that you wage within aren't meant to be lost,
I'll be your light & make you win, no matter even if you exhaust.

Let's sail all the oceans of guilty chaos ghosting within,
and shower ourselves with love bracing the burning hearts and skin,
Listen to my roar and unfurl me giving a hint of your blush,
I can recognize the champion of my soul emerging into my only crush.

~~Love~~ Soulful Bites

"The moment was then discovered lost in youth. I fell for him and witnessed the truth."

29. Mystic Dawn

The shades of grey nights covered and cuddled us,
We remained hugged hovering over the chills of mystic dawn,
I felt every depth of thrills of being in love under my limbs,
His entrance into my life made the wind beneath my wings.

The tingling warmth of his fingertips,
Rolled over to feel my lustrous lips,
He fancied every drop of my oral dew,
Which made my nerves twitch and all my senses blew.

He invaded my soul and captured my senses,
Set me off, from all my pathos and distress,
He claimed ownership over my spirit and body,
Healed the scars and my agony like nobody.

~~Love~~ Soulful Bites

"I felt like I was trapped and partly consigned. With all the new definitions of love that he has defined."

30. Oasis of Serenity

I sometimes wonder and stuck myself in awe,
He is that mirror reflection of all the images I draw,
I have always prayed for the love so warm and new,
God has showered his blessings in the shape of you.

The love in my heart is to be showered in many ways,
An epoch of love is ought to be created in all our coming days,
This intimacy among us inspired me in real such,
Wanting to travel through the bliss of his love and touch.

Now I don't mourn any loss of life,
He is sent to fulfill all the craziness I drive,
I guess the oasis of serenity is now drenched so below,
Now I nap and rest assured of true love.

Visions of fantasies are no longer meant to hide....
Embracing ourselves in love and soulful bites.....

- Udaigiri Amaravathi

TO READ MORE WORKS OF THE AUTHOR
CHECK OUT HER OTHER BOOK

Unquenchable Desires

You can find this book on
Amazon, Flipkart and our Website
(Scan to check out the book)

www.ingramcontent.com/pod-product-compliance
Lightning Source LLC
LaVergne TN
LVHW030324070526
838199LV00069B/6557